Perfecting the art of ennui

Charlotte Roberts

BookLeaf Publishing

Presentation by *BookLeaf Publishing*

Web: www.bookleafpub.com

E-mail: info@bookleafpub.com

ISBN: 978-93-95755-98-6

First edition 2022

Perfecting the art of ennui

I used to think that ennui meant
Doing things without intent

I've always been a perfectionist
Drawing up plans and ticking off lists

Overachieving and outperforming
Highlighting and brainstorming

It's starting to become a bore
Every task is now a chore

That's what my perfection was
Working hard just for the boss

But hold on, wait! Let's turn this around
I need to do what's never been allowed

It's time I compartmentalise
Before my soul inside me dies

I need a new perfection now
As much as my time will allow

Hearing the birds chirp and tweet
A musical sound that's ever so sweet

It's hygge and it's feng shui
Listening to Nina and Louis

My ennui now at last has meaning
Spending hours just daydreaming

Reading, writing and taking rest
My ennui moments are the best

Fairy lights

Warm gold stars are trickling down
Softening my sorrowed frown

I feel at last I can relax
No dissociative panic attacks

Leaving behind a sorry day
And letting my mind just drift away

Drift away into nothingness
Anything else is just hopeless

In a transcendental state
A calm new world my mind can create

Silence is my only friend
As time stands still to slowly mend

Slinking down to stare at the light
At least for now I know I'm alright

Mindlessness

Mindfulness means exactly that
A busy head full of stress and chat
It forces you to think and do
And people expect so much of you

To me the goal is mindlessness
Where I can relax and decompress
To be without a thought or pressure
And quietly enjoy a simple pleasure

Watching fish swim all around
And Autumn leaves fall to the ground
Raindrops racing down the glass
And clouds are waving as they pass

I think you've got a bit mixed up
Of how to best refill your cup
So try and empty out your head
And take a lie down on your bed

Then you just might understand
Just how much of life is bland
Perhaps just take some time to rest
You'll find your life is much less stressed

Amateur creative

I want to be a writer
Creating poems and plays
Running through storylines
Daydreaming for days
My life as inspiration
It's imitating art
A therapeutic method
To heal my broken heart

I want to be an artist
Quirky and unique
Sculpting crazy models
Like my skeleton punk freak
Sketching and painting
I can lose hours
Arranging a mural
Of cellophane flowers

I want to be a performer
Singing on the stage
My favourite memories
Of when I came of age
Building up my confidence
In the City Hall and Playhouse
Inhibiting a character
And raising eyebrows

I want to be a photographer
Capturing different stills
Of everyday life
Like gnomes on window sills
Experimenting with angles
And focus and contrast
Monochrome looks best
As if it's from the past

I want to unleash myself
I want to be me
Before I end up on the shelf
As empty as can be

Yoga

Tree pose keeps me grounded
A person who is more well rounded
Finding balance

Compartmentalise work and home
Spending time to write a new poem
Creating balance

Taking time to rest and play
Therapeutic routine for every day
Living in balance

Classical recovery

Sinking into my pillow
While listening to the magic

With closed eyes, I feel it deeply
My body responds to every sound

My fingers twinkle with pianos
My toes dance with violins

Creating strong mental imagery
Both dramatic and quaint

Quiet, gentle voices at each interim
The only way to start a morning now

I look forward to each day now
Easing through the darkness

Cups of tea

Every now and then
On a day we're both free
I'll shoot the breeze with my friend
Over a cup or two of tea

Catching up on life
Our work and personal plights
Discussing world events
And putting it all to rights

Picking up where we left off
It's like no time has passed
Since the last time that I saw her
When we sat and gassed

Even though we're still young
There is no better way
Than chatting by the teapot
For us to spend the day

Clouds

Every time I see the beauty
I'm always taken by surprise
By the early morning sky
A lone bird flies

Slowly drifting by
Like colourful cotton wool
A free entertainment show
A moment never dull

Remembering when I was little
Spending hours gazing
Finding funny images
With the sunlight blazing

I rush to get my camera
To capture the view
Immortalised forever
So I can show you

Autumnal evening

Drip drops causing tiny cascades on the ground
Showering a lonely flower

Twinkling down on my hand like falling stars
It feels like sparks of heat

A sound that encapsulates the air
Crescendos and hushes that crash all around

Long thin beams of light falling down from the
sky
Little beads gathering on the washing line

There's an honesty in rainfall
Gentle and tough

I'd watch it for hours
Standing at the back door

Mid century modern

Hepburn and Monroe
Barstow and Sillitoe

Kitchen sink dramas
Short pinstripe pyjamas

Mod dresses and shoes
Rhythm and blues

Feminine mystique
Asymmetric chic

Miniskirts
Paisley shirts

Holy trinity of rock
Monochrome and colour block

Carnaby Street
Merseybeat

Babycham
Silver Cross pram

Mary Quant
Cursive font

Vinyl records
Vespas and surfboards

Mini Cooper
Hula Hooper

John and Paul
Sindy doll

Kaleidoscope eyes

Anxiety comes in many ways
In the night as well as the days

For some it just feels physical
For others it's far less typical

In moments when I feel unsafe
And I can't feel my feet on the ground

My eyes can play tricks on me
The colours fade and swirl all around

Kitchen sink drama

Angry young men
Like Jimmy and Arthur
Vic too, I guess
When each became a father

Poor sad girls
All with a baby
None of them planned
Better off without them, maybe

Why does it always seem to be
That parenthood for youth causes such misery?

What were their dreams?
What were their plans?
More than just arguing
While washing the pans

From the French meaning

What is in a name?

Womanly: flirtatious, hour glass and glamorous

Quiet: intuitive, reflective and introverted

Artistic: experimental, creative and quirky

Strength: in character, mind and soul

Free thinking: non-conformist, unconventional and individualistic

Do not underestimate her. She knows what she is doing.

Summer

Flowers in the park
With people having picnics
Perfect summer's day

Drum tobacco

I know you're still around me
There's no doubt that it's you
The strong scent of your tabs
Gives me the biggest clue

Even for a moment
I know I can't be wrong
Walking around the house
Is right where you belong

I hope and wish that every day
I still can make you proud
You know my thoughts and feelings
Though I don't say them out loud

I see you in my dreams
Like nothing's even happened
But then reality hits
When I wake and life is blackened

I've got so much to tell you
And a lot of things left unsaid
I wish I could go outside
And find you working in the shed

It still feels weird to think
That it even happened at all
I still get shivers when I remember
How you made your curtain call

Praise song for a legend

You were
A child to me
Laughing and playing and wondering

You were
A woman to me
Flaunting and flirting and teasing

You were
An icon to me
Shining and smiling and pioneering

You were
The face of the angels to me
The symbols femininity to me
The star of a golden era to me
                              Dreaming and
dreaming

I guess I am a fantasy, you said

New beginnings

The past is over
The days are done
I'm happy that I'm happy
The sadness has gone

My life is changing
There's no stopping me
I'm excited to find out
What it's to be

For me, a new version
A beaming smile
So clear on my face
You could see it a mile

Embracing the things
Both big and small
That help me go forward
And make me stand tall

Music therapy

The distant sound of
A twinkling piano:
Best relaxation

Ode to June

Bohemian girl
A flower child
Like a rainbow

I wish I could have been like you
I wish I was allowed to be

You - free as a bird
Me - stunted growth

I think of a life
I could have had
No, I need to stop
It's just too sad
Maybe in another life
In a different world
I could be a better me
A little flower girl

Wildflowers

Wild spirits need to be nurtured
Intuitive to the vibes
Let go of the old tired ways of life
Don't conform if it feels wrong
Freedom to choose what I do with my life
Love the uniqueness of the self
Others may not get it, that's fine
Work without play will kill my soul
Enjoy my quirkiness
Rainy days help me bloom
Sadness doesn't scare me

Benson

I only knew you
For seventeen years
Every spring I relive
My worst nightmares

My world turned upside down
In such a short time
Causing so much pain
It should be a crime

Nicknames and play fights
Are things that I miss
Talking about places
Where we would find bliss

Each time I hear
A motorbike roar
It reminds me of you
My heart hits the floor

I often see you
In my dreams
Like nothing's changed
So it seems

I learned so much
But still lots to know
It doesn't seem fair
That you had to go

I'm becoming more like you
In so many ways
Your memory brings the sun
On my stormiest days